Stag Hunt

after Cranach

Norbert Krapf

THE SCEPTRE PRESS

Knotting . Bedfordshire

I

On an island of green
the plumed, costumed lords
in leather saddles
on muscular horses
charge straight ahead
with lances leveled.

Bucks & does
break from cover.
Hounds snap at
their hoofs as they
flee toward the river.

With his antlers
a surrounded stag gores
a hound in the gut,
and with his back leg
kicks in the head.

II

Antlers bob across
the roiling river
like clusters of driftwood.
Hounds dogpaddle behind.

In the bushes
on the bank
on the other side,
bearded huntsmen crouch
& aim their crossbows
at the stags
whose hoofs have
just touched bottom.

In a thicket
a slain stag
slie on his side.
His red tongue spills
like blood onto the ground.
A spaniel nuzzles
into his crotch.

III

From the spired town
in the background,
a boat floats around
the bend into the scene.

Lords & ladies
in long pleated gowns
& broad hats stand
chatting in the middle.

In the stern, a friar
paws at a lady whose
bosom is heaving.
In the bow, a lady
sits playing a violin
while a wounded stag
thrashes out of the water.